LISBON
THE CITY AT A GLANCE

GW00836094

Museu Nacional do Azulejo
A former convent finished in 1509, this
museum is dedicated to traditional Por
tile design. The shop sells reproduction
as contemporary ceramics.
Rua da Madre de Deus 4, T 21 810 0340

Graça
Standing out in this church-heavy district
is the curvaceous Panteão Nacional (Campo
de Santa Clara, T 21 885 4820). If it's open,
visit the dome, overlooking the Tagus below.

Castelo de São Jorge
After checking out the view from the castle,
walk down the cobbled streets to Baixa
listening to fado, the Portuguese lament that
drifts out of the windows in the old town.
Rua de Santa Cruz, T 21 880 0620

Coliseu dos Recreios
Take in a performance at this 19th-century
music hall, which is still a major venue today.
Rua das Portas de Santo Antão 96, T 21 324 0580

Sé Catedral
Visit this iconic church, originally completed
in 1147, before a rustic brunch at the Pois café
(Rua São João da Praça 93-95, T 21 886 2497).
Largo da Sé, T 21 886 6752

Baixa
Each street in this grid-like shopping district
has a speciality, including the buttons and
traditional Bilros lace of Rua da Conceição.

Chiado
Listen to a jazz session at São Luiz Teatro
Municipal (Rua António Maria Cardoso 38, T 21
325 7640) or opera at Teatro Nacional de São
Carlos (Rua Serpa Pinto 9, T 21 325 3000).

INTRODUCTION
THE CHANGING FACE OF THE URBAN SCENE

The Romans knew what they were doing when they first settled in Lisbon atop the seven hills overlooking the grand Tagus River. Portugal's capital provides an enchanting first impression: the blazing yellow light that glints off its cobblestoned streets, the faded glamour of centuries-old establishments that still exist in their limestone-finished edifices, and, of course, the glittering river views that often appear when you're least expecting them. The city is one of Europe's oldest and most enchanting, yet there is a modern, beating heart beneath Lisbon's romantic facade.

Despite Portugal's recent economic troubles, its biggest city is resolutely facing the future without forgetting its rich past. While national culture is fiercely held on to, from food to fado, Lisbon's well-travelled residents are capitalising on their craft expertise and business nous. New design studios, smart shops, exquisite hotels and cutting-edge architectural projects all give plenty of space and respect to the heritage of a city that is changing fast, thanks in part to an influx of migrants from Europe and beyond.

Although Lisbon's various tribes do not tend to mix well, and the latest hotspots – from secret beaches to clandestine bars and restaurants – are often known only to locals, it is possible for the visitor to cut through these boundaries and enjoy all there is to offer. It's just that in this city full of hidden gems, you really have to know where to look, and that's where we come in.

ESSENTIAL INFO
FACTS, FIGURES AND USEFUL ADDRESSES

TOURIST OFFICE
Lisbon Welcome Center
Praça do Comércio
T 21 031 2810
www.visitlisboa.com

TRANSPORT
Airport transfer to city centre
The Carris Aerobus departs every 20
minutes between 7am and 10.30pm
Car hire
Europcar
www.europcar.com
Metro
www.metrolisboa.pt
Taxis
Teletáxis
T 21 811 1100
Cabs can be hailed in the street
Tourist card
A three-day Lisboa Card (€39) grants free
travel and free entry to most attractions
Trams
www.carris.pt

EMERGENCY SERVICES
Emergencies
T 112
Late-night pharmacy
Farmácia Correia de Azevedo
Rua Luís de Camões 42b
T 21 363 8625

EMBASSIES
British Embassy
Rua de São Bernardo 33
T 21 392 4000
www.gov.uk/government/world/portugal
US Embassy
Avenida das Forças Armadas
T 21 727 3300
portugal.usembassy.gov

POSTAL SERVICES
Post office
Praça Luís de Camões 20
T 21 322 3701
Shipping
UPS
T 70 723 2323
www.ups.com

BOOKS
**Architecture in Lisbon and the South
of Portugal since 1974** by Carsten Land,
Klaus J Hucking and Luíz Trigueiros (Blau)
Lisbon: What the Tourist Should See
by Fernando Pessoa (Shearsman Books)

WEBSITES
Art/Design
www.artecapital.net
www.stick2target.com
Newspapers
www.clix.pt
www.publico.pt

EVENTS
ExperimentaDesign
www.experimentadesign.pt
Lisbon Architecture Triennale
www.trienaldelisboa.com

COST OF LIVING
**Taxi from Portela Airport
to city centre**
€13
Cappuccino
€3.50
Packet of cigarettes
€4
Daily newspaper
€2
Bottle of champagne
€40

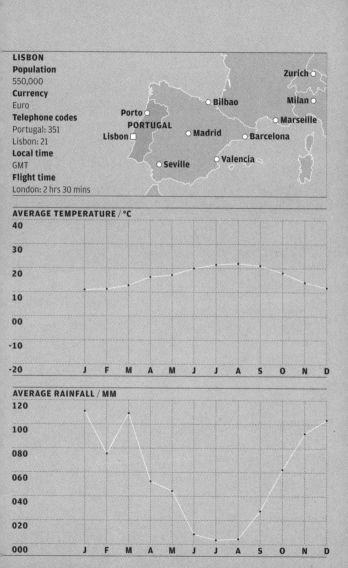

LISBON
Population
550,000
Currency
Euro
Telephone codes
Portugal: 351
Lisbon: 21
Local time
GMT
Flight time
London: 2 hrs 30 mins

Zurich ○
Milan ○
○ Bilbao
Porto ○ ○ Marseille
PORTUGAL
Lisbon □ ○ Madrid ○ Barcelona
○ Seville ○ Valencia

AVERAGE TEMPERATURE / °C

40											
30
20
10
00
-10
-20	J	F	M	A	M	J	J	A	S	O	N	D

AVERAGE RAINFALL / MM

120											
100
080
060
040
020
000	J	F	M	A	M	J	J	A	S	O	N	D

NEIGHBOURHOODS

THE AREAS YOU NEED TO KNOW AND WHY

To help you navigate the city, we've chosen the most interesting districts (see below and the map inside the back cover) and colour-coded our featured venues, according to their location; those venues that are outside these areas are not coloured.

PARTE ORIENTAL
The mid-20th-century town-planning schemes of Olivais Norte and Sul aren't without interest, but the biggest attraction here has to be Parque das Nações, site of the World Expo '98. One of the largest urban redevelopment projects in Europe, it's now a feast of modern architecture.

GRAÇA/ALFAMA
In the shadow of Castelo de São Jorge (see p009), Lisbon's historic quarters of Alfama, Castelo and Graça are where the city was born. It is a wonderfully atmospheric maze of cobbled streets, old houses and lovely churches stretching down to the Tagus at Santa Apolónia.

AMOREIRAS/CAMPO DE OURIQUE
A mix of offices and residential quarters, this area is as much about high-profile landmarks, like the Torres das Amoreiras (see p009), as hidden gems, such as Jardim das Amoreiras and its charming museum, Fundação Arpad Szenes-Vieira da Silva (Praça das Amoreiras 56, T 21 388 0044).

RESTELO/ALCÂNTARA
This district boasts tropical gardens, well-heeled residents, several impressive historic monuments, including Padrão dos Descobrimentos (see p012), and Lisbon's cultural pole, Centro Cultural de Belém (see p012). Across the tracks on Avenida de Brasília, the Museu da Electricidade (T 21 002 8190) doubles as a jet-set hangout.

LAPA/SANTOS
Once-fashionable Lapa is where most embassies can be found, whereas Santos is home to independent shops, such as O Epicurista (Largo do Conde Barão 49, T 21 396 0990) and Domo (Largo de Santos 1g, T 21 395 5328), as well as the Museu Nacional de Arte Antiga (see p027).

AVENIDAS NOVAS
The 1879 Avenida da Liberdade was the city's first wide, central avenue, paving the way for the Avenidas Novas — long, axial boulevards linking downtown Lisbon to Campo Grande (and these days, the airport). Design-conscious citizens lust after the spacious 1950s apartments here.

BAIRRO ALTO/CHIADO
Nightlife quarter Bairro Alto looks out over neighbouring Chiado, which survived the 1988 fire and 10-year reconstruction to become the city's most stylish district. Traditional shops like A Carioca (see p086) have been joined by an abundance of hip boutiques, such as Soulmood (see p084).

MONSANTO
Dubbed 'Lisbon's lung', this 10 sq km park area's insalubrious reputation has undergone a transformation thanks to many 'green' and security initiatives. It's still not the most comfortable place to get a flat tyre after 10pm, but during the day most inhabitants are joggers, cyclists or squirrels from the nearby ecological park.

LANDMARKS
THE SHAPE OF THE CITY SKYLINE

Lisbon is compact and relatively easy to navigate, provided you remember that when the Avenidas Novas were created, the wide boulevards opened up in a V shape from Chiado (downtown). They run in sequence and link to the north and north-east of the city. The other main artery follows the train track by the river, and links east to west. Lisboans delineate the areas along the avenues by referencing the handiest square or garden, although these spots often have unofficial names. The most significant are in Baixa: Terreiro do Paço is the alias for Praça do Comércio, whereas Praça Dom Pedro IV is known as Rossio. In much of the city, except for the upper Avenidas Novas and Parte Oriental, getting disoriented in the maze of narrow streets is an enjoyable part of the experience.

Fortunately, there is a good stock of landmarks to steer you right, the most obvious being the majestic Ponte 25 de Abril (see p014). Mosteiro dos Jerónimos (Praça do Império, T 21 362 0034) is Belém's cornerstone, and the Torres das Amoreiras (Avenida Engenheiro Duarte Pacheco) loom over the capital. The Portuguese parliament, Palácio de São Bento (Praça de São Bento), and Praça de Touros do Campo Pequeno (Praça do Campo Pequeno, T 21 799 8450) gave their names to their quarters; Castelo de São Jorge (T 21 880 0620) overlooks Baixa, Alfama and Graça; and Estação do Oriente (overleaf) forms the centrepiece of the World Expo '98. *For full addresses, see Resources.*

Estação do Oriente

This station, built for the World Expo '98, won Santiago Calatrava the 1999 Brunel Award for railway architecture. It is the most recognisable structure in the area courtesy of its flamboyant metallic and laminated glass roof, which is always beautifully lit at night. However, locals advise against standing on the windy platforms whenever the weather is bad.
Avenida Dom João II

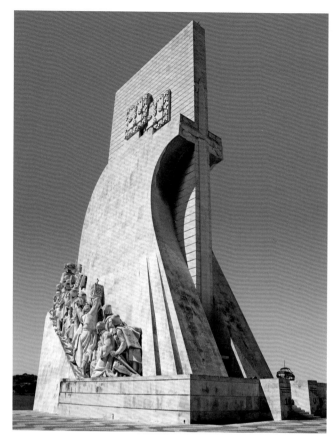

Padrão dos Descobrimentos

One of Lisbon's great symbols, this was the only temporary construction created for the Exposição do Mundo Português in 1940 that was made permanent. The rest of the exhibits were taken down, some bulldozed, and the Centro Cultural de Belém (T 21 361 2400) is now located here. The 52m-high Padrão dos Descobrimentos (Monument to the Discoveries) was built in wood to the designs of Cottinelli Telmo, the exhibition's main architect, and the sculptor Leopoldo de Almeida. This concrete replacement was inaugurated in 1960 to honour the 500th anniversary of the death of Henry the Navigator. To the front of the statue, the dates of his discoveries are set in metal on a map of the world made from multicoloured marble by Luís Cristino da Silva.
Avenida de Brasília, T 21 303 1950

Nossa Senhora do Rosário de Fátima
Opened in 1938 and designed by local architect Porfírio Pardal Monteiro, this is the only modernist church in town, far removed from the usual overload of golden plaster and tiling that springs to mind with the words 'Lisbon church'. Built from cement, it features work by some of the most noted artists of the time, including Francisco Franco's low-relief figures on the facade, and José Sobral de Almada Negreiros' stained-glass panels throughout the various chapels, the apse and the choir. Stunning in its serenity, openness and sense of reclusion, Igreja de Nossa Senhora do Rosário de Fátima is the most welcoming church in Lisbon. It is open daily from 8.30am to 1pm and from 4pm to 8pm. *Avenida Marquês de Tomar, T 21 792 8300, www.paroquiansrfatima.com*

Ponte 25 de Abril

Built by the American Bridge Company in 1966 and originally named after the Portuguese dictator António de Oliveira Salazar, this suspension bridge crossing the Tagus River was renamed after the Carnation Revolution, which started on April 25 1974. Taking almost four years to construct, it was, on completion, the longest central span in Europe. The rust-red bridge has a total length of roughly 2.28km, and is longer than its common associative reference, San Francisco's Golden Gate, although it was, in fact, modelled on Frisco's other main crossing, the San Francisco to Oakland Bay toll bridge. In 1999, two railway tracks were added, but we would recommend driving across it southbound for sweeping views of the Tagus estuary on one side, and the Grande Lisboa bays on the other.

HOTELS

WHERE TO STAY AND WHICH ROOMS TO BOOK

Over the past decade or so, Lisbon has become an unexpectedly glamorous destination. Various international hotel groups have recognised its potential; Design Hotels member Memmo Alfama (Travessa das Merceeiras 27, T 21 351 4368) opened here in 2013, a property that gears its concierge services to its beautiful Moorish locale. Then there's the revamped Sheraton (Rua Latino Coelho 1, T 21 312 0000), which has also made a significant impact on the scene. With a constantly growing number of new venues, it has become difficult to recognise the best – the International Style Four Seasons Hotel Ritz (see p026) is our trustworthy favourite.

However, if you know your way around, you'll feel spoilt for choice. Central hotels such as Bairro Alto (see p018), Hotel do Chiado (Rua Nova do Almada 114, T 21 325 6100), renovated by Álvaro Siza Vieira, and The Beautique Hotels Figueira (Praça da Figueira 16, T 21 049 2940) all have definite staying power. Venture a little further from the beaten track and you'll find charming residential suites at Palácio Ramalhete (see p030); contemporary riverside boltholes such as Altis Belém (see p019); and grand hilltop *palácios* like Pestana Palace (see p022). The unashamedly decadent should head to Palácio Belmonte (Patéo Dom Fradique 14, T 21 881 6600), and Paris is writ large at the Heritage Avenida Liberdade (Avenida da Liberdade 28, T 21 340 4040).

For full addresses and room rates, see Resources.

Fontecruz

Set among the high-end boutiques and restaurants of Avenida da Liberdade, this 72-room hotel is housed in a Pombaline building renovated by local architect José Vaz Pires in 2012. The dark, glass-clad exterior is one of the most contemporary on the grand boulevard, and the rooms have panoramic vistas of the surrounding commercial and sightseeing areas. Features such as the Moet & Chandon Bar and a 15m-high screen near the lobby make Fontecruz one for those who are partial to a bit of flashiness. Add to this the orange and olive trees in the courtyard, where breakfast is also served, and the vintage trunks and chaises longues in rooms such as the White Suite (above), and you have a playful addition to Lisbon's hotel scene.
Avenida da Liberdade 138-142,
T 21 041 0000, www.fontecruzhoteles.com

Bairro Alto Hotel

This central, cosmopolitan hotel opened back in 2005 and its top-floor terrace, which has an amazing river view, and the restaurant Flores do Bairro (T 21 340 8252) quickly became an integral part of the Chiado scene. Housed in a restored 18th-century building, Lisbon's very first boutique property is, aesthetically, as you would expect, a mix of contemporary and classic styles. Designed by Grace Leo-Andrieu with Porto's Bastidor, the ground floor is all about space and clarity, and features Moroccan tiles on the walls. The single rooms face Praça Luís de Camões (ask for No 307), whereas your best bet for a double is the Corner Suite 406 or one of the handsome Prestige Rooms (above), which look out on to the Tagus. *Praça Luís de Camões 2, T 21 340 8288, www.bairroaltohotel.com*

Altis Belém Hotel & Spa

Developed by Portuguese architects Risco, this modern creation is the only hotel in the city to sit right on the banks of the Tagus estuary. The building's exterior, wonderfully textured by large wooden shutters, is perpendicular to the dock, but positioned so that the view between the Torre de Belém (Avenida Brasília) and the Padrão dos Descobrimentos (see p012) isn't obstructed. All rooms use bold white and grey tones, in keeping with the drama of the structure, and the Diplomatic Suites (above and overleaf) have balconies and panoramic views of the Tagus (if you're not too busy using the spa, that is). The two restaurants offer outdoor seating, and Bar 38° 41' (T 21 040 0210) integrates perfectly with the riverside promenade. *Doca do Bom Sucesso, T 21 040 0200, www.altishotels.com*

Diplomatic Suite Premier, Altis Belém

Pestana Palace

High on a hilltop in Alcantâra, the Pestana is set in the 19th-century neoclassical Valle Flôr Palace, a former residence of the nobility, which is now classified as a national monument. Although the hotel may be a touch formal, the beautifully restored main building (Green Room, right) is one of the cosiest places in the city to have tea and cake on a winter's afternoon. By far the best rooms are the four Royal Suites; our favourite is Don Manuel I. Don't miss the fantastic view over the river and Ponte 25 de Abril (see p014) from the veranda, and for an even better vista, head up to the rooftop of the ex-coach house, now the hotel's conference centre, which can be found just across the street.

Rua Jau 54, T 21 361 5600, www.pestana.com

Lapa Palace

Constructed in grand splendour by the Count of Valenças in 1883, Olissippo Hotels' Lapa Palace has retained many charming details following the restoration of its contemporary wing in 2003. These include the lush garden around the pool, ceramics and paintings by the Bordalo Pinheiro brothers, the tower and several imposing function rooms, including the 50-capacity Sala Columbano (opposite). Rooms on the fifth floor are decorated with furniture from the old palace, and the pick of the bunch is the Suite Conde de Valenças (above), originally part of the ballroom, which has restored gold leaf on its walls, two vast mirrors and a great view of the still prestigious neighbourhood. Restaurante Lapa has a Mediterranean menu, and the poolside Le Pavillon serves lunch and cocktails in summer.
Rua do Pau da Bandeira 4, T 21 394 9494, www.lapapalace.com

Four Seasons Hotel Ritz

Usually, the Portuguese overrate foreign influence and devalue anything linked to Salazar, head of the toppled dictatorship. But if he had designed a hotel it might well have looked exactly like the Ritz. The building by Portuguese architect Porfírio Pardal Monteiro, the public areas by French interior designer Henri Samuel and the five Foundation Suites featuring pre-20th-century Portuguese furniture are all that remain of the original 1959 Ritz, yet they are more than enough for modernist fans to feel at home. The elegant Imperial One Bedroom Suites (above) feature three spacious terraces, as well as views over Parque Eduardo VII and, on the higher floors, the Tagus River. Be sure to make use of the spa (see p094).
Rua Rodrigo da Fonseca 88, T 21 381 1400, www.fourseasons.com/lisbon

As Janelas Verdes

This former royal residence is right next to the Museu Nacional de Arte Antiga (T 21 391 2800) and has just 29 rooms (No 24, above), making it a restful choice for those who prefer serene city living. The intimate reception rooms, including the Library (overleaf), are filled with books and objets d'art, evoking the air of a genteel private home, and the rooftop terrace has a riverside view that rivals those at other hotels in the centre. Over the years it has housed several noted residents, such as the Count of Sabugosa and the 19th-century novelist and master of realism Eça de Queirós, who wrote *Os Maias* here, basing the magical abode in the story on the building. If it's good enough for him, it's good enough for us.
Rua das Janelas Verdes 47, T 21 396 8143, www.asjanelasverdes.com

Palácio Ramalhete
Comprising only 12 suites, this hideaway in
the smart Janelas Verdes neighbourhood
is a prime example of Lisbon's knack for
restoration, particularly of its Pombaline
buildings. The 18th-century detail in the
rooms, such as wood-lined walls, stucco
ceilings and original fireplaces, evokes a
grandeur tempered by the friendly, down-
to-earth service. Ramalhete's highlight
is its charming, 300 sq m multi-level
patio, complete with a pool and a variety
of lovingly cared-for plant life. The Dove
Room (left) and the Oak Room are the
most unique of the 12 that are available;
the former used to be the palace's chapel
and features original azulejos and old
wood flooring, the latter has floor-to-
ceiling oak panelling and river views.
*Rua das Janelas Verdes 92, T 21 393 1380,
www.palacio-ramalhete.com*

24 HOURS

SEE THE BEST OF THE CITY IN JUST ONE DAY

This one-day itinerary by no means incorporates all there is to discover in Lisbon, but it does provide a glimpse into a small and captivating capital that still likes to surprise. Culinary treasures, breathtaking sights and a creative heart await those willing to scratch the city's surface. Have breakfast at Padaria São Roque bakery (opposite), before walking down the road to take in an unrivalled eastward view of the city. After a window-shopping meander in Bairro Alto's cobbled streets, arrive in Chiado for more individual stores, including A Vida Portuguesa (see p034).

Head to The Decadente (Rua São Pedro de Alcântara 81, T 21 346 1381) for an impressively refined lunch on the ground floor of a hostel. Loop back to Chiado, and walk a little further downhill to the stop for tram No 15, which passes the Ponte 25 de Abril (see p014) on its way to Belém, where you can scope out the splendid art collection of the Museu Coleção Berardo (see p035). Tuck into a couple of *pastéis de nata* (here, *pastéis de Belém)* at the famous Antiga Confeitaria de Belém (Rua de Belém 84-92, T 21 363 7423), to fuel a tour of the national monuments, then make your way to Appleton Square (see p036) for a niche display of Portuguese art. Complete your day back in the centre with a memorable meal prepared by one of the country's best-known chefs at the Michelin-starred Belcanto (see p038).

For full addresses, see Resources.

10.00 Padaria São Roque

In a city full of *pastelarias* (pastry shops), some majestic and legendary, others stark and understated, Padaria São Roque is our favourite. An alluring place for breakfast, this old working bakery, founded in 1840, has an art deco interior as charming as the staff who serve the freshly baked bread and pastries here. Animal-themed azulejos on the bar and marble pillars that stretch up to the intricate ceiling provide a grand setting for a *bica* (similar to an espresso) and a sandwich, or some of the coconut-topped *pão de Deus* ('God's bread'). Order at the counter, or grab a seat at one of the few prized tables outside. Then, once you are refuelled, walk out, turn right and take in the captivating view from the Miradouro de São Pedro de Alcântara gardens.
Rua Dom Pedro V 57, T 21 322 4356

11.30 A Vida Portuguesa

Local entrepreneur Catarina Portas opened this store back in 2007 with the purpose of championing classic 'made in Portugal' stock, while also harnessing the national affection for exquisitely packaged, quality lifestyle products. A shrine to beloved, yet often elusive, Portuguese items such as Claus Porto soaps and Bordallo Pinheiro porcelain swallows, this is a must-see for visitors.

Customers range from elderly Lisbon ladies whose Alantoíne hand cream has all but disappeared from other stores to fine art students stocking up on their Serrote notebooks. A Vida Portuguesa has spawned many copycats in the city, but brand exclusives and the knowledgeable staff here keep it firmly at number one.
Rua Anchieta 11, T 21 346 5073, www.avidaportuguesa.com

13.00 Museu Coleção Berardo

This museum, housed in the Vittorio Gregotti and Manuel Salgado-designed Centro Cultural de Belém, is the place to go for a contemporary art fix, especially if you don't have time to explore Lisbon's assortment of smart galleries. Regular shows display the acquisitions of Joe Berardo, a businessman, speculator and mega-collector, whose passion for 20th-century and early 21st-century modern art includes the usual suspects – Warhol, Magritte, Picasso, Bacon – as well as homegrown heavyweights such as Pedro Cabrita Reis, Jorge Molder and Paula Rego. The grand exhibitions cover major movements, including pop art, surrealism and minimalism, and there are also tours and workshops on offer. Closed Mondays.
Praça do Império, T 21 361 2878,
www.museuberardo.com

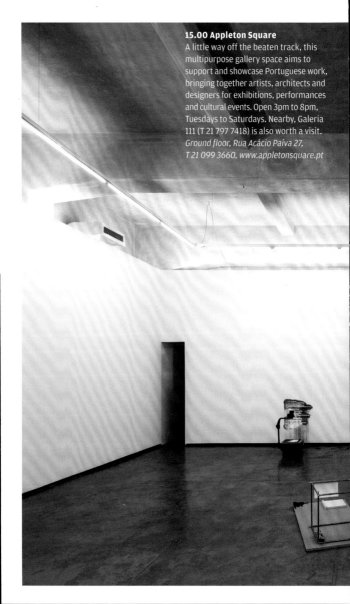

15.00 Appleton Square
A little way off the beaten track, this multipurpose gallery space aims to support and showcase Portuguese work, bringing together artists, architects and designers for exhibitions, performances and cultural events. Open 3pm to 8pm, Tuesdays to Saturdays. Nearby, Galeria 111 (T 21 797 7418) is also worth a visit.
Ground floor, Rua Acácio Paiva 27, T 21 099 3660, www.appletonsquare.pt

20.00 Belcanto

In a well-heeled corner of Chiado, inside a sober space that was once a private bar (and brothel), José Avillez, the rising star of new Portuguese dining, serves up Michelin-starred molecular gastronomy. Originally opened in 1958, Belcanto was refurbished when Avillez took over, and relaunched in 2012. Twenty-two chefs feed a 50-person capacity, their menu incorporating delicate foam explosions and witty presentations delivered with (occasionally saccharine) flair. Dishes like Skate Jackson Pollock (skate with green olive, cuttlefish ink, and a carrot sauce, served with an image of Pollock's *No 8*) can cause smirking, but there is plenty of substance beneath the styling. Closed Sundays, Mondays and bank holidays. *Largo de São Carlos 10, T 21 342 0607, www.joseavillez.pt*

URBAN LIFE
CAFÉS, RESTAURANTS, BARS AND NIGHTCLUBS

In a city that takes its time, eats late, and parties later, even on a school night, Lisbon evenings almost always merge into the early morning. A playground for royal exiles back in the 1940s, and for sailors long before that, the capital has a well-deserved reputation for lazy summer days followed by balmy, raucous nights.

The industrial-chic riverfront club Lux Frágil (see p052) still draws the party crowd, but locals have also been discovering the joys of dancing in smallish venues, such as Lounge (Rua da Moeda 1, T 21 397 3730) and late-night cultural spaces like Zé dos Bois (see p060). Bairro Alto remains the main starting point for a night out, but the city's numerous *miradouros* (viewpoints) now host screenings, DJ sets and concerts for the post-work crowd.

During daylight hours, Lisbon has always lived, worked and breathed in its cafés, while in the evenings, dining out is taken very seriously. The re-imagining of the dockside Kais (see p058) and the sprawling charm of Casa Independente (see p054) have made way for innovative restaurateurs, with chefs such as José Avillez at Cantinho do Avillez (Rua dos Duques de Bragança 7, T 21 199 2369) paying attention to classic Portuguese fare. Lisbon's gastronomy scene is coming of age, and the escalating ubiquity of street food and Michelin stars have revealed both a commitment to heritage and genuine love for all that is foreign, shiny and new. *For full addresses, see Resources.*

SushiCafé Avenida

Portugal and Japan have a long shared history, so it's no surprise that Japanese-inspired cuisine features prominently in Lisbon's cosmopolitan neighbourhoods. One of four SushiCafé restaurants in the city, Avenida opened in 2011, and here chef Daniel Rente combines Japanese specialities with fresh local ingredients, using molecular techniques to guarantee the wow factor. Creative dishes such as

Wagyu beef carpaccio served with foie gras snow and chocolate, or the Gindara Goma (black cod with sprouts, mashed black-eyed peas, *nimono* and black sesame sand) are enough to distract diners from the slightly harsh lighting design. Open 12.30pm to 3.30pm for lunch, and from 7.30pm for dinner. *Rua Barata Salgueiro 28, T 21 192 8158, www.sushicafe.pt*

Bica do Sapato
Actor John Malkovich, Manuel Reis of Lux Frágil (see p052) and Fernando Fernandes of restaurant Pap'açorda (T 21 346 4811) have turned this riverside warehouse into a sleek restaurant with minimalist decor that evokes a 1960s airport departure lounge. The menu is a modern take on traditional fare. *Armazém B, Avenida Infante Dom Henrique, T 21 881 0320*

Restaurante Galeto

This 24-hour diner-style haunt is a tough nut to crack. It doesn't lure you in – in fact, at first glance the waiters behind the dark wood counter don't seem very welcoming at all. Designed in 1966 by Victor Palla and Bento de Almeida back when the country was a dictatorship, it has one of the most fantastic vintage interiors in the whole city. The trick is to match its stiff attitude with a laidback resolve. Once seated at one of the high stools against the long counters (there are no traditional tables here), you're fine. Order the hamburger, the biggest and best in town, and if you don't have a glass of *groselha* (gooseberry juice), you'll definitely be missing out.
Avenida da República 14, T 21 354 4444

Tivoli Sky Bar

Another favourite with locals, the Sky Bar at the Tivoli Lisboa hotel (T 21 319 8900) on the scenic Avenida da Liberdade is one of the city's best vantage points for pre-dinner drinking and corporate shoulder-rubbing – its spacious terrace faces downtown towards the Arco Triunfal. First impressions of the cocktail menu might make you cringe, but despite their names, concoctions such as Girl From Ipanema (cachaça, mango, passionfruit, lime, sugar) and the Elixir of Life (Rémy Martin XO, Grand Marnier, lemon, sugar) are ideal for a rooftop sundowner. Salads and sharing plates are available, as is an extensive wine/aperitif list. Sky Bar is open from 5pm daily, and for brunch on weekends from 11am, April to October. *Avenida da Liberdade 185, T 21 319 8832, www.tivolihotels.com*

Taberna da Rua das Flores

Hailing from Porto and having previously worked the kitchens at Lisbon's luxurious Clube de Jornalistas (T 21 397 7138), respected chef André Magalhães went back to basics when he joined business partners Bárbara Matos and Adriano Jordão to open this 25-seat tavern in an old Chiado barbershop. Portuguese staples – olive oil, pâté, cheese – are displayed in cabinets and available to buy, whereas the daily changing menu celebrates unusual national fare (bull's feet, barnacles), as well as seafood and meat dishes of the highest calibre: the ceviche is a must. The commitment to the best of Portuguese cuisine combined with the hectic atmosphere and rustic decor, by way of salvaged furniture, make this an authentic pitstop. Closed Sundays. *Rua das Flores 103, T 21 347 9418*

Orpheu Caffé

Although it is named after the short-lived magazine conceived by the early 20th-century poet Fernando Pessoa, this café/bar is destined for longevity. Welcomed by aficionados of Lisbon's burgeoning breakfast scene, Orpheu offers light meals and an outdoor seating area at the back for a lazy summer brunch. Its late hours (it's open until midnight from Tuesday to Saturday) and proximity to Bairro Alto also make it an ideal pre-party spot in which to share a bottle of Douro amid lovingly restored wooden furniture and chandeliers, and floral wallpaper that keeps it cool, not kitschy. On Sundays, start your day here with a leisurely breakfast before visiting the small organic market located just outside in the centre's most charming gardens. *Praça do Príncipe Real 5a, T 21 804 4499*

Pedro e o Lobo
This former gallery is a favoured venue of well-heeled locals and curious travellers. The chefs, Nuno Bergonse and Diogo Noronha, have devised a menu of deceptively simple seasonal dishes, which complement the decor, by owner and architect Luis Baptista, who has integrated wood, concrete and glass into the sophisticated space.
Rua do Salitre 169, T 21 193 3719

Noobai Café

Among Lisbon's most familiar features are its plentiful outdoor seating areas surrounded by painted iron fences, known as *esplanades*. It's rare to come across a café or restaurant that doesn't have one. Noobai boasts two, both with stunning views of the river, and a colourful, relaxed beach-style bar (above) serving a healthy international menu of dishes, such as crusted cod with nuts and spices. The venue provides blankets for customers who want to watch the sun set on cooler evenings while listening to one of the occasional live DJ sets or the constant soundtrack of fado, bossa nova or jazz. We suggest doing so with a glass of the excellent sakerinha (caipirinha with sake). Open from noon and closed Mondays.
Miradouro do Adamastor, T 21 346 5014, www.noobaicafe.com

Galeria Miguel Nabinho

PEDRO CALAPEZ
PEDRO CALAPEZ
PEDRO PROENÇA
RUI SANCHES
ANA JOTTA
MANUEL BOTELHO
NOÉ SENDAS
MIGUEL ANGELO ROCHA
JOSÉ LUIS NETO
RUI MOREIRA
LUISA CUNHA
ANDRÉ GONÇALVES
GAETAN
JEMIMA STEHLI
SANCHO SILVA
SANTIAGO CUCULLU

ENTRADA...

PRATO...

E... 2 GALER

Cervejaria da Esquina

In a corner building in the quiet Campo de Ourique neighbourhood, to which few tourists venture, is Cervejaria da Esquina, the brainchild of celebrated chef Vítor Sobral. The place excels in popular seafood dishes given mildly inventive reworks, and the plates of razor clams, shrimps, scallops and lobster are simply but tastefully presented from a busy integrated kitchen; desserts such as Gorreana green-tea flan add an inspired touch. There is also an interesting selection of *cervejas* (beers) that go beyond the usual Sagres/Super Bock options, including *esquininha* (a small cup of extremely fresh beer). Eating crab here, straight out of the shell, is an absolute pleasure. Closed Mondays. *Rua Correia Teles 56, T 21 387 4644, www.cervejariadaesquina.com*

Lux Frágil

This three-floor clubbing behemoth on the Santa Apolónia docks has, despite losing a little of its ice-cool reputation in recent years, maintained an unwavering commitment to eclectic musical curation, proudly keeping the flag flying for the global electronic revolution. As with any club that's been around for this long (it opened in 1998), the decor is a little dated in some areas, but the soundtrack – house, techno and leftfield live concerts being the main draw – renders Lux the place to be most weekends. The rooftop bar is the perfect spot for lounge breaks on summer nights. We suggest checking the venue's website before going, to see who's in town for a mammoth set, although it is best avoided completely on Saturdays. Expect queues for big-name events.
Armazém A, Avenida Infante Dom Henrique, T 21 882 0890, www.luxfragil.com

Casa Independente

This popular eaterie on the edge of the increasingly popular Mouraria area serves unfussy Portuguese and Mediterranean fare, such as salads and fish dishes, using ingredients sourced from producers in the city and the wider region. During the day, most customers while away hours on laptops inside or on the terrace, and the furnishings – originally found in the former *palacete* (mansion) – create an early 20th-century shabby-chic ambience. Casa Independente stages weekly concerts by Lisbon-based indie groups and hosts parties at the weekends. The three owners (Patrícia Craveiro Lopes, Inês Valdez and Joana Nóbrega) also collaborate with local businesses to reappropriate abandoned gardens for more own-food sources.
Largo Intendente Pina Manique 45, T 21 887 5143, www.casaindependente.com

Bistro 100 Maneiras

The cuisine in this contemporary dining space was dreamed up by award-winning Yugoslav Ljubomir Stanišić, now known as one of Portugal's best chefs. He launched its predecessor in Cascais and is famed for his work at nearby 100 Maneiras (Rua do Teixiera 35), the more upmarket sister restaurant that serves only one thing: an ingeniously developed 10-course tasting menu. In Bistro 100, the food is mainly designed for sharing and incorporates Portuguese tastes, including meat and fish dishes, as well as a range of influences from Stanišić's travels. Choose a cocktail or sample one of the four new wines that Stanišić has devised in collaboration with Dirk Niepoort, whose family has been in the winemaking business since 1842. *Largo da Trindade 9, T 910 307 575, www.restaurante100maneiras.com*

Fábulas
It's hard to get a table at this relaxed space, where lounging for hours is the norm. The café features original Singer tables complete with sewing machines, and vintage furniture and 200-year-old arches link the dining room to the gallery, which has exhibitions curated by print studio Contraprova (T 91 843 3884). *Calçada Nova de São Francisco 14, T 21 601 8472, www.fabulas.pt*

Kais

Lisbon has been undergoing a frenzy of renovation over the past decade, and the abandoned buildings on the docks are particularly sought after by ambitious developers. Kais is one of the most ingenious projects – a late 19th-century tram warehouse transformed into a modern temple of fine dining. Designer Maria José Salavisa, citing Frank Lloyd Wright as a key inspiration, has deftly accentuated the high ceilings, exposed brick and original ironwork with grand lighting and splendid details, including indoor olive trees and a waterfall. The menu is international: try the Mozambican prawn curry and then the chocolate trilogy with coffee gravy. Although, to be honest, anything tastes good in this setting.
Cais da Viscondessa, Rua da Cintura, T 21 393 2930, www.kais-k.com

Largo

Largo combines the talents of three Lisbon innovators: architect and designer Miguel Câncio Martins, chef Miguel Castro e Silva and owner Frederico Collares Pereira, known in the city for his Doca Seis and Doca Peixe restaurants. The interiors, designed by Martins, may appear to lean towards oceanic chintz at first glance, but the effect soon becomes mesmerising. In the main dining room, three large black glass panes are cut into a 30m wall, with jellyfish swimming amid blue and green lighting. The food here is much simpler than the decor, but by no means less striking – we recommend the tagliolini with spicy tomato sauce, shrimps and mussels, followed by sole fillets with scallops in a thyme and leek sauce.
Rua Serpa Pinto 10a, T 21 347 7225, www.largo.pt

Zé dos Bois
Live music, exhibitions, multidisciplinary performances and a double life as a nightclub enables the non-profit ZDB, based above a bookshop, to draw an eclectic crowd. The bar (pictured) opens on to a courtyard that leads into the venue, and a large window means you can sit outside and still see the acts. The rooftop is used for summer screenings.
Rua da Barroca 59, T 21 343 0205

INSIDER'S GUIDE

MARCO BALESTEROS, DESIGNER AND PUBLISHER

Originally from Évora in Alentejo, Marco Balesteros has been living in Lisbon since he was 18. Co-founder of Random Press publishers and design studio Letra (www.letra.com.pt), he likes to start his day with a coffee at Martinho da Arcada (Praça do Comércio 3, T 21 887 9259) or Casa Chinesa (Rua do Ouro 274, T 21 342 3680). 'Both have good selections of confectionery,' he says, 'although if you want great *pasteis de nata*, choose Martinho.'

Aware of the intricacies of Lisbon's cultural scene, Balesteros says highlights include The Barber Shop (Rua Rosa Araújo 5), a small space focusing on artistic research and ephemeral projects, and Carpe Diem (Rua do Século 79, T 21 197 7102; open 1pm-7pm), a gallery and artistic residence in a former Bairro Alto palace. For a quick bite, he recommends the daily food market on Largo Martim Moniz, which is close to central downtown. 'The area has a nice mix of cultures,' he says, 'and this main square is the place to go for tacos, sushi or just a beer.' When it comes to regional cuisine, Balesteros rates nearby Zé da Mouraria (Rua João do Outeiro 24, T 21 886 5436) 'for its *bacalhau na brasa* [roasted cod]'.

Late nights often end with a drink at Viking Bar (Rua Nova do Carvalho 7, T 21 342 6468), in the somewhat seedy Cais do Sodré neighbourhood – a former playground for randy sailors that now boasts bars and restaurants as well as after-hours clubs. *For full addresses, see Resources.*

ARCHITOUR
A GUIDE TO LISBON'S ICONIC BUILDINGS

The Lisboan authorities have not been proactive about protecting architecture that's too recent to be deemed 'historical'. Only a few modernist churches, monuments and schools remain faithful to their original purpose. Happily, it seems the tide is shifting, with idiosyncratic renovations such as the 1950s art deco <u>Cinema São Jorge</u> (Avenida da Liberdade 175, T 21 310 3400), or the iconic <u>Casa dos Bicos</u> (Rua dos Bacalhoeiros, T 21 880 2040), which reopened as the HQ of author José Saramago's foundation in 2012. In spite of the abundance of 18th-century churches, antediluvian districts and old-France styled avenues, Lisbon also has plenty to offer in terms of modern urban gawping. The most challenging structures in town used to be at the World Expo '98 site (see p010), but it's starting to look a little redundant compared with the likes of Aires Mateus' <u>EDP HQ</u> (Praça Marquês de Pombal 12), Centro Ismaili (see p068) and Charles Correa's <u>Champalimaud Centre</u> (see p072).

Looking ahead, projects over the next few years include a new riverside complex by Renzo Piano on the site of a former arms factory, and another design by Norman Foster that's potentially being drawn up for Santos. But, considering the track record of previous ambitious plans (the promenade extension from Praça do Comércio to the Ponte 25 de Abril took much longer than expected), Lisboans will only believe the hype once a building is complete. *For full addresses, see Resources.*

Escola Superior de Música

This music school, part of the Instituto Politécnico de Lisboa, was designed by local architect João Luís Carrilho da Graça with the aim of creating a well-insulated, practical building that also reflects the diversity of its students. Completed in 2008, the huge central space references the structure of a cloister, while the walls gently slope to incorporate the size and scope of the instruments being practised inside. Concrete is omnipresent throughout the 16,900 sq m site, utilised for its solidity and sound insulation, and the indoor and outdoor areas are merged together with understated integrity. It's difficult to catch a glimpse of the action inside, as there are few windows, but you might take a peek through the glass at the corners.

Campus de Benfica, Instituto Politécnico de Lisboa, T 21 322 4940, www.esml.ipl.pt

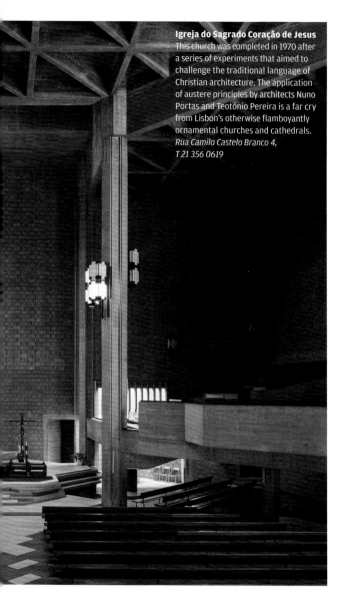

Igreja do Sagrado Coração de Jesus
This church was completed in 1970 after a series of experiments that aimed to challenge the traditional language of Christian architecture. The application of austere principles by architects Nuno Portas and Teotónio Pereira is a far cry from Lisbon's otherwise flamboyantly ornamental churches and cathedrals.
Rua Camilo Castelo Branco 4,
T 21 356 0619

Centro Ismaili

Architect Raj Rewal, who worked with Frederico Valsassina Arquitectos, found inspiration in a variety of sources for this commission by the Aga Khan Foundation for its Portuguese HQ, completed in 1998. Persian gardens, Granada's Alhambra, Agra's Fatehpur Sikri Mughal monument and even Lisbon's Mosteiro dos Jerónimos are all paid homage in the geometric design. Six courtyards and an external garden are landscaped with running water and local foliage, and although the first floor is reserved for the work of the institution, visitors are free to wander around the ground-floor spaces through open-air pathways. Located some way from the centre, in São João, this is a gem that's too often overlooked.
Rua Abranches Ferrão, T 21 722 9000, www.theismaili.org

Hotel Vitória

Cassiano Branco, one of Portugal's 20th-century starchitects, designed this marble-clad building, which was completed in 1936. Originally residential apartments, 10 years later it was expanded and opened as a hotel, which was used by the Nazi secret service as a base during WWII. Now, ironically, the Vitória is home to the HQ of the Communist Party of Portugal. Admire its uniform circular balconies from street level; unfortunately the topmost roof terrace, complete with pergola, is not open to the public, but you can still visit most of the interiors if you ask nicely. It's worth it to see the art deco details and opulent rooms up close. Alongside Branco's Teatro Eden (Praça dos Restauradores 24), this is one of the most iconic modernist buildings in all of Lisbon.
Avenida da Liberdade 170

Universidade Nova de Lisboa

The rectorate building of Lisbon's newest university (founded in 1973) was designed by Aires Mateus, probably the most inspired architectural firm in the country today. The slender tower houses west-facing offices, its geometrically random windows overlooking Parque Monsanto. Limestone was used for the walls, the public square they frame and the grand steps leading up to the contemporary *praça*. Large-scale foyers, meeting rooms and auditoriums are set at the base of the building. Completed in 2001, the structure won Portugal's Valmor Prize for Architecture the next year. Even the modern creations over at the World Expo '98 site can barely compete with its sense of drama. *Campus de Campolide, T 21 371 5600, www.unl.pt*

Champalimaud Centre for the Unknown

Designed by Charles Correa and opened in 2010, this biomedical research centre boldly expresses the essence and mood of its surroundings. Housing state-of-the-art laboratories, auditoriums, a cancer centre and Darwin's Café (T 21 048 0222), it also boasts wall-enclosed gardens with soft apertures revealing the sky. Walkways behind the building integrate with the waterfront, and pedestrians and cyclists can cross the public spaces to the sites of Belém. The element of the 'unknown' is accentuated with a path rising through the main curved buildings towards two columns that border an infinity-style pool of water, extending at the point where the Tagus meets the Atlantic. The sense of mysticism is typical of the Indian architect.
Avenida Brasília, T 21 048 0200,
www.fchampalimaud.org

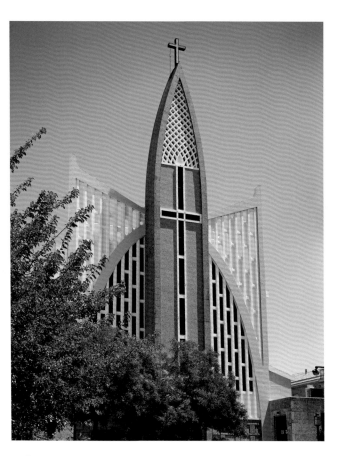

Igreja de Nossa Senhora Auxiliadora

Perhaps *the* architectural treat in Lisbon, not so much for the fantastic, bold sword-like facade that towers high above the rooftops, nor for its midcentury colour scheme and lines, but for the interior. Absurdly characteristic of 1960s Lisbon, it was designed in 1964 by João Simões, as the city itself was expanding to the upper Avenidas Novas and beyond. The architect utilised the very same modern materials that were being used to build the new apartment blocks. It might not look or feel like a real church, but that, in this case, is a compliment.
Praça de São João Bosco 34

Fundação Calouste Gulbenkian

This beautiful concrete structure, which was completed in 1969 and designed by Ruy Jervis Athouguia, Pedro Cid and Alberto Pessoa, hosts the art collection of Fundação Calouste Gulbenkian, a private institution with interests in arts, charity, education and science. Comprising two galleries, a library and an auditorium that seats about 1,200, as well as outstanding interior spaces, the building is surrounded by Jardim Calouste Gulbenkian, which was created by António Viana Barreto with Gonçalo Ribeiro Telles, Portugal's most well-known landscape architect. The gardens include an outdoor amphitheatre and are an ideal escape from the busy city. Visit for exhibitions, conferences and educational programmes. Closed Mondays. *Avenida de Berna 45a, T 21 782 3000, www.gulbenkian.pt*

Teatro Thalia

Portuguese architect Gonçalo Byrne, together with Patrícia Barbas and Diogo Seixas Lopes, converted the ruins of this neoclassical theatre in 2012. Inaugurated in 1843, the Thalia was built for the Count of Farrobo, an aristocrat and party animal (the Portuguese expression, *forrobodó*, is used to describe a shindig that gets out of control), but by the time a fire burned down most of the building in 1862, the count had lost his fortune. The site was unused for nearly 150 years before its reincarnation, in which the remains were covered by a shell of terracotta concrete and extended on to a glass pavilion to form a multipurpose space for musical events and performances. The interiors are untouched, yet the overt juxtaposition of old and new is surprisingly harmonious. *Estrada das Laranjeiras 197, T 21 781 1600*

Pavilhão de Portugal

Lisbon's only publicly accessible building (besides the Hotel do Chiado, see p016) by Portugal's most famous architect, Álvaro Siza Vieira, is closed and has an uncertain future. But it is arguably the one Siza construction you don't have to go inside to enjoy. Created for the World Expo '98, the pavilion's design is based on a sheet of paper balancing on two bricks. Standing beneath the amazing thin concrete pall that seemingly floats between the lateral structures, you are in the best part of the Pavilhão. The strong colours of the tiles add to the experience, as do the other buildings in the Parque das Nações, such as Peter Chermayeff's Oceanário (T 21 891 7002) and Santiago Calatrava's Estação do Oriente (see p010).
Alameda dos Oceanos

SHOPPING

THE BEST RETAIL THERAPY AND WHAT TO BUY

Although the northern city of Porto has been giving Lisbon's retail landscape a serious run for its money, the capital is beginning to catch up again, with well-presented and diverse options standing out amid the unfortunate boom in tourist tat. The streets around Avenida da Liberdade are still the place for high-end shopping, while Chiado has a little bit of everything. Here, highlights include Paris em Lisboa's linens (Rua Garrett 77, T 21 342 4329), porcelain from Vista Alegre (Largo do Chiado 20-23, T 21 346 1401) and handmade gloves at Luvaria Ulisses (see p082).

Nearby Bairro Alto is not quite as good for artsy or alternative shopping as it used to be, although Galeria de Exclusivos (Rua da Rosa 195-197) is great for independent local fashion and music. Up the hill, Praça do Príncipe Real is a hub of stylish clothes boutiques: Alexandra Moura MA+S (Rua Dom Pedro V 77, T 21 314 2511) and Kolovrat 79 (Rua Dom Pedro V 79, T 21 387 4536) are just two must-visits, and the area is also home to a handful of original design stores, including BCT (Praça do Príncipe Real).

Aside from fashion and homewares, Lisbon's shopping scene still has plenty to offer. Avid record collectors will enjoy Matéria Prima (Rua da Rosa 197, T 21 096 5104) or Discolecção (Calçada do Duque 53a, T 21 347 1486), and bookworms should venture out to Alcântara for the impressive Ler Devagar (see p083).

For full addresses, see Resources.

Conserveira de Lisboa

A shop dedicated solely to selling tinned sardines may seem like an unlikely kind of business but, since 1930, Conserveira de Lisboa has enjoyed a flourishing trade thanks to its colourfully packaged and enticingly stacked goods, most of which are emblazoned with the female face of historic Portuguese brand Tricana. The Ferreira family, who have run the tiny store since it opened, have recently diversified into canned cod, octopus, anchovies, tuna (Tricana fillets, above, €18.95 for 1.8kg) and a variety of pâté and condiments. If this is all a little too fishy for your tastes, the products' retro-souvenir value is irresistible; each tasty selection of tins is lovingly wrapped up for you in brown paper and string at the counter. *Rua dos Bacalhoeiros 34, T 21 886 4009, www.conserveiradelisboa.pt*

Luvaria Ulisses

With room for just one customer at a time, this is the smallest shop in Lisbon. Although gloves are no longer the central fashion accessory they were in 1925 when this bijou store opened, Luvaria Ulisses remains unfazed and continues to stock its vitrine with retro-looking apparel of its own design. All the original fixtures remain, so it's worth visiting just to see the empire-inspired decor, but if you are in the business of buying new gloves, ask for a 'peccary' model; they're handmade and kept at the back for the best clients. Naturally, purchasing a pair still comes with the pampering ritual of a personal fitting, complete with talcum-powder spray, a massage and a delightful little pillow on which to rest your elbow.
Rua do Carmo 87a, T 21 342 0295, www.luvariaulisses.com

Ler Devagar

Located in Alcântara's LX Factory – a former thread and fabric manufacturing complex dating to 1864, now a creative hub offering everything from fashion to food – bookshop Ler Devagar ('read slowly') fills a large, industrial space. Although the organisation can be a little muddled, there's a vast range: from arts and technology to the great lusophone novelists and much in-between, in several languages. The store plays host to a busy schedule of cultural events such as book launches and concerts amid the towering shelves. There's also an Asian restaurant, Malaca Too (T 967 104 142), a bar on the ground floor, which opens until 2am at weekends, and café Bolo da Marta (T 918 929 654) on the first floor.
G-03, Rua Rodrigues Faria 103,
T 21 325 9992, www.lerdevagar.com

Véronique

Located in the same building as the minimal womenswear store Soulmood (T 21 346 3179), Véronique Laranjo's space stocks the latest collections by European brands, alongside vintage accessories. It's a stylish selection, as you would expect from a former adviser for several high-end labels including Joseph, Prada and Marc Jacobs.
Travessa do Carmo 1, Loja 5, T 21 195 2299

A Carioca

As you walk through Chiado, the smell of freshly ground coffee wafts out of the doors of small venues. Among these is the flamboyant A Carioca, which dates from the 1930s. It was bought in the 1990s by venerable roasting company Negrita, and the overhaul that followed restored the little art deco deli to its former glory. Even the old grinding machine is still in use, although sadly not often enough on the rare and renowned arabica beans from the African island of São Tomé. If you are not lucky enough to drop by when it's in stock, the Gorreana green tea, grown on the Azores islands using traditional processes, is an excellent second choice. Chocolate from former Portuguese colonies and jars of retro-packaged sweets make nice take-aways. *Rua da Misericórdia 9, T 21 342 0377*

Caza das Vellas Loreto

This wood-panelled shop has been open since 1789 and is an enchanting gateway to the past. Centuries ago, the area around Praça Luís de Camões used to be full of candlemakers, but this is now one of the only ones left in Portugal. Don't blink as you walk in, or you might miss the small, peculiar front window that is part medieval, part chocolate box. The cosy interior is filled with candles – displayed in soaring glass cabinets, and all handmade by Caza das Vellas Loreto using time-honoured methods. Every customer gets undivided attention here, and processing a transaction takes as long as is required. There are a multitude of scents to choose from and the selection is at its best in the months leading up to Christmas; the beeswax varieties are our favourites.
Rua do Loreto 55, T 21 342 5387

SPORTS AND SPAS
WORK OUT, CHILL OUT OR JUST WATCH

The construction frenzy that preceded Portugal's hosting of Euro 2004 didn't do that much for Lisbon. The architecture of the two stadiums built for Benfica and Sporting Clube de Portugal, the city's top football teams, isn't especially interesting. So any desire to watch the beautiful game is best satisfied by a trip to Estádio do Restelo (Avenida do Restelo, T 21 198 0000), home of the third-ranked team, Belenenses. The river views from the north stand compensate for any less-than-stellar moves on the pitch.

City hall is slowly but surely improving conditions for cyclists, who can now cruise uninterrupted along the waterside from Praça do Comércio to Belém, thanks to refreshed cycle paths. It's also worth renting a bicycle and heading to Monsanto, where 20km of gravelled lanes traverse the forest hilltop. Elsewhere, the blue-blooded showjumping and dressage centre Hipódromo do Campo Grande (see p090) is a great place to learn, practise or just watch.

The sleek rooftop fitness centre at the Four Seasons Hotel Ritz (see p026) offers stunning views over Lisbon and boasts a 400m running track, as well as a sumptuous spa (see p094); although the facility run by local fashion duo Alves/Gonçalves (opposite) could soon become the deluxe choice. Academia Life Club (Rua da Cintura do Porto a Santos, Armazém J, T 21 393 4020) and Longevity Wellness Spa (see p092) are relaxed alternatives.

For full addresses, see Resources.

Alves/Gonçalves

A powerhouse in both Portuguese mens- and womenswear, Manuel Alves and José Manuel Gonçalves are a couple who get top billing whenever ModaLisboa (Lisbon's fashion week) comes around. For their own spa, right in the heart of the capital, they have enhanced the contemporary interiors with personal vintage finds (as well as furniture by Charles Eames and Established & Sons) to create a soft and subtle setting for this haven of well-being. The duo rely on hard-to-find brands such as Leonor Greyl and Mavala to seduce a stylish clientele, and hairstyling, massages, facials and manicures are all part of the luxe package. The typically late opening hours (until 10pm) are especially useful for any last-minute beauty emergencies. *20 Travessa Guilherme Cossoul, T 21 346 0690, www.alvesgoncalves.com*

Hipódromo do Campo Grande
It's not a racecourse these days but a showjumping and dressage venue, and home to century-old Sociedade Hípica Portuguesa (Portuguese Equestrian Society). Global events, including the CSIO (Lisbon International Official Show Jumping), are attended by upper-crust locals and Hollywood royalty alike.
Off Alameda da Cidade Universitária,
T 21 781 7410, www.sociedadehipica.pt

Longevity Wellness Spa

The Corinthia Hotel's out-of-the-way location, near Parque Monsanto, renders it slightly impractical for guests who want to explore the centre. However, it suits the spa perfectly, allowing for space and tranquility that's hard to find downtown. The hotel group is renowned throughout Europe for its impressive retreats and this is no exception; featuring a jacuzzi, sauna, ice fountain, Turkish bath and 16 therapy rooms. Alongside Elemis facials, massages and body treatments, there are also 'medical solutions and aesthetic medicine' on offer. We can't comment on the Botulinum Toxin, but the Comfort Foot Ritual (complete with pedicure) works wonders on weary soles beaten by the city's cobblestoned streets.

Avenida Columbano Bordalo Pinheiro 105, T 21 723 6305, www.corinthia.com

Four Seasons Hotel Ritz Spa
After a few circuits of the hotel's rooftop
jogging track or partaking in a class at
the fitness centre, we suggest a visit
to its 1,500 sq m basement spa. Relax in
the eucalyptus steam room and try one
of the Espa treatments, before you enjoy
a meal by the indoor lap pool (pictured)
as you gaze out over Parque Eduardo VII.
*Rua Rodrigo da Fonseca 88, T 21 381
1400, www.fourseasons.com/lisbon/spa*

ESCAPES

WHERE TO GO IF YOU WANT TO LEAVE TOWN

Lisbon doesn't lack for good escapes. But in a city where driving 30km for late-afternoon tea, a dip in the sea or an after-dinner coffee is the norm – and that's on a weekday – it's hard to define escape. It helps that the place is surrounded by beautiful beaches and quirky villages. And then there's the weather, which Lisboans always love to complain about, despite the special sunlight that bathes the city for at least seven months of the year.

The capital has the advantage of being roughly at the centre of Portugal. Travelling times have been reduced by the recent highway linking north and south and by a network of airports. And although TAP (www.flytap.com), Portugal's flagship carrier, is an underdog at Portela Airport, where foreign airlines are favoured, it's your best option for domestic flights.

We considered sailing lessons in the Southwest Alentejo and Vicentine Coast Natural Park (T 28 332 2735), some 100km south of Lisbon; and we daydreamed about the Álvaro Siza Vieira-designed spa at the Vidago Palace Hotel (Parque de Vidago 16, Vidago, T 27 699 0900) in the Douro Valley. But we have decided to be bolder. We propose a trip to self-enclosed cabin retreat Casas Na Areia (opposite), surrounded by Comporta's heavenly landscape, a day in the enchanting Sintra (see p098), and a visit to Évora's L'And Vineyards (see p100) to experience enotourism at its chicest. *For full addresses, see Resources.*

Casa Na Areia, Comporta

This modern eco-escape, an hour's drive from Lisbon, comprises two old masonry buildings and two contemporary structures by Portuguese architect Manuel Aires Mateus. Opened in 2010, the retreat sleeps roughly eight people, cabins are made from local materials, such as straw and wood, and a small lap pool overlooks the rice fields of Comporta. Sand-carpeted floors in the communal House 0 (above) inject the right amount of mellow into a space that's as stylish as it is laidback, and there's even underfloor heating to warm up the sand during winter nights. Borrow one of Areia's bikes for the 20-minute ride to an 80km stretch of tranquil beach, the Porto Palafita fishing dock, or the handful of nearby restaurants.
Sítio da Carrasqueira, T 93 441 8316, www.casasnaareia.com

Sintra

Lord Byron described Sintra as a 'glorious Eden', and that was before King Fernando II dreamed up the Palácio Nacional da Pena (right; T 21 910 5340), which kickstarted the construction of other palaces of a similar fervour in the vicinity. Sintra was consequently deemed the first centre of European romantic architecture and has since been designated a UNESCO World Heritage Site. We suggest arriving early, visiting Pena and the Freemason haven of Quinta da Regaleira (T 21 910 6650), then enjoying a picnic of shrimp rissoles and *travesseiros* (traditional pastries) from Piriquita (T 21 923 0626) set in the gardens of the Palácio de Monserrate (T 21 923 7300). End your day with tea and tasty *queijadas* (cheese pastries) at Sapa (T 21 923 0493). It's best to avoid Sintra at the weekends and on national holidays, when crowds of tourists descend.

L'And Vineyards, Alentejo

Situated 100km from Lisbon, this country club and hotel is set around a vineyard and offers sublime views of the medieval hilltop castle of Montemor-o-Velho. There are just 22 suites; the 10 Sky View options (No 10, above) all feature private gardens with plunge pools and retractable roofs, taking advantage of one of Europe's least light-polluted areas. The interiors, including the spa, were designed by architect Marcio Kogan, who utilised materials such as slate and wood for a sleek aesthetic; and the reception building is a modern translation of Roman and Arabic atrium architecture. Wine tours and tastings are available daily, and the nearby UNESCO World Heritage Site of Évora is also worth a stopover. *Estrada Nacional 4, Herdade das Valadas Montemor-o-Novo, Évora, T 26 624 2400, www.l-andvineyards.com*

Casa das Histórias, Cascais

Housing the paintings and drawings of London-based artist and Portuguese icon Paula Rego, Casa das Histórias was designed by Eduardo Souto de Moura, who was selected by Rego herself for the project. Located in the seaside town of Cascais, 30km west of Lisbon, this 'house of stories' was completed in 2009. The Porto-born architect took inspiration from local construction techniques to create the arresting terracotta pyramid structures, and the lush green surroundings have also been incorporated into the interiors to welcoming effect. This is arguably one of Souto de Moura's finest works; the other being the 1998 Manoel de Oliveira cinema house in Porto.
Avenida da República 300, T 21 482 6970, www.casadashistoriaspaularego.com

NOTES
SKETCHES AND MEMOS

RESOURCES
CITY GUIDE DIRECTORY

A

A Carioca 086
Rua da Misericórdia 9
T 21 342 0377

A Vida Portuguesa 034
Rua Anchieta 11
T 21 346 5073
www.avidaportuguesa.com

Academia Life Club 088
Rua da Cintura do Porto a Santos
Armazém J
T 21 393 4020
www.academia-lifeclub.pt

Alexandra Moura MA+S 080
Rua Dom Pedro V 77
T 21 314 2511

Alves/Gonçalves 089
20 Travessa Guilherme Cossoul
T 21 346 0690
www.alvesgoncalves.com

Antiga Confeitaria de Belém 032
Rua de Belém 84-92
T 21 363 7423
www.pasteisdebelem.pt

Appleton Square 036
Ground floor
Rua Acácio Paiva 27
T 21 099 3660
www.appletonsquare.pt

B

Bar 38° 41' 019
Altis Belém Hotel & Spa
Doca do Bom Sucesso
T 21 040 0210
www.altishotels.com

The Barber Shop 062
Rua Rosa Araújo 5
www.thisisthebarbershop.blogspot.co.uk

BCT 080
Praça do Príncipe Real
www.bct.pt

Belcanto 038
Largo de São Carlos 10
T 21 342 0607
www.joseavillez.pt

Bica do Sapato 042
Armazém B
Avenida Infante Dom Henrique
T 21 881 0320
www.bicadosapato.com

Bistro 100 Maneiras 055
Largo da Trindade 9
T 910 307 575
www.restaurante100maneiras.com

Bolo da Marta 083
G-03
Rua Rodrigues Faria 103
T 918 929 654

C

Cantinho do Avillez 040
Rua dos Duques de Bragança 7
T 21 199 2369
www.cantinhodoavillez.pt

Carpe Diem 062
Rua do Século 79
T 21 197 7102
www.carpediemartepesquisa.com

Casa dos Bicos 064
Rua dos Bacalhoeiros
T 21 880 2040
www.josesaramago.org

Casa Chinesa 062
Rua do Ouro 274
T 21 342 3680

HOTELS
ADDRESSES AND ROOM RATES

Altis Belém Hotel & Spa 019
  Room rates:
  double, from €240;
  Diplomatic Suite, from €750;
  Diplomatic Suite Premier, from €950
  Doca do Bom Sucesso
  T 21 040 0200
  www.altishotels.com

As Janelas Verdes 027
  Room rates:
  double, from €160;
  Room 24, from €160
  Rua das Janelas Verdes 47
  T 21 396 8143
  www.asjanelasverdes.com

Bairro Alto Hotel 018
  Room rates:
  double, €230;
  Room 307, from €180;
  Prestige Room, €350;
  Corner Suite 406, €430
  Praça Luís de Camões 2
  T 21 340 8288
  www.bairroaltohotel.com

The Beautique Hotels Figueira 016
  Room rates:
  double, from €130
  Praça da Figueira 16
  T 21 049 2940
  www.thebeautiquehotels.com

Casa Na Areia 097
  Room rates:
  cabin, from €500
  (three-night minimum stay)
  Sítio da Carrasqueira
  Comporta
  T 93 441 8316
  www.casasnaareia.com

Hotel do Chiado 016
  Room rates:
  double, €110
  Rua Nova do Almada 114
  T 21 325 6100
  www.hoteldochiado.com

Fontecruz 017
  Room rates:
  double, from €140;
  White Suite, from €475
  Avenida da Liberdade 138-142
  T 21 041 0000
  www.fontecruzhoteles.com

Four Seasons Hotel Ritz 026
  Room rates:
  double, €345;
  Imperial One Bedroom Suite, €2,050
  Rua Rodrigo da Fonseca 88
  T 21 381 1400
  www.fourseasons.com/lisbon

Heritage Avenida Liberdade 016
  Room rates:
  double, €150
  Avenida da Liberdade 28
  T 21 340 4040
  www.heritageavliberdade.com

L'And Vineyards 100
  Room rates:
  suite, from €170;
  Sky View Suite, €215
  Estrada Nacional 4
  Herdade das Valadas
  Montemor-o-Novo
  Évora
  Alentejo
  T 26 624 2400
  www.l-andvineyards.com

Lapa Palace 024
  Room rates:
  double, from €285;
  Suite Conde de Valenças, €2,500
  Rua do Pau da Bandeira 4
  T 21 394 9494
  www.lapapalace.com
Memmo Alfama 016
  Room rates:
  double, from €115
  Travessa das Merceeiras 27
  T 21 351 4368
  www.memmoalfama.com
Palácio Belmonte 016
  Room rates:
  double, from €500
  Páteo Dom Fradique 14
  T 21 881 6600
  www.palaciobelmonte.com
Palácio Ramalhete 030
  Room rates:
  double, from €175;
  Dove Room, €275;
  Oak Room, €290
  Rua das Janelas Verdes 92
  T 21 393 1380
  www.palacio-ramalhete.com
Pestana Palace 022
  Room rates:
  double, €200;
  Dom Manuel I Suite, €1,500
  Rua Jau 54
  T 21 361 5600
  www.pestana.com
Sheraton 016
  Room rates:
  double, €145
  Rua Latino Coelho 1
  T 21 312 0000
  www.sheratonlisboa.com

WALLPAPER* CITY GUIDES

Executive Editor
Rachael Moloney

Editor
Ella Marshall
Authors
Claudia Saraiva
Syma Tariq

Art Director
Loran Stosskopf
Art Editor
Eriko Shimazaki
Designer
Mayumi Hashimoto
Map Illustrator
Russell Bell

Photography Editor
Elisa Merlo
Assistant Photography Editor
Nabil Butt

Chief Sub-Editor
Nick Mee
Sub-Editors
Farah Shafiq
Vicky McGinlay

Editorial Assistant
Emma Harrison

Interns
Soo Ah Chung
Elisabetta D'Addario
Olivia Hellewell
Inês Rainho de Azevedo

**Wallpaper* Group
Editor-in-Chief**
Tony Chambers
Publishing Director
Gord Ray
Managing Editor
Oliver Adamson

Wallpaper* ® is a
registered trademark
of IPC Media Limited

First published 2007
Revised and updated
2011 and 2014

All prices are correct at
the time of going to press,
but are subject to change.

Printed in China

PHAIDON

Phaidon Press Limited
Regent's Wharf
All Saints Street
London N1 9PA

Phaidon Press Inc
180 Varick Street
New York, NY 10014

Phaidon® is a registered
trademark of Phaidon
Press Limited

www.phaidon.com

A CIP Catalogue record for
this book is available from
the British Library.

All rights reserved.
No part of this publication
may be reproduced, stored
in a retrieval system or
transmitted, in any form
or by any means,
electronic, mechanical,
photocopying, recording
or otherwise, without
the prior permission of
Phaidon Press.

© 2007, 2011 and 2014
IPC Media Limited

ISBN 978 0 7148 6648 2

PHOTOGRAPHERS

Luís Ferreira Alves
Casa das Histórias,
pp102-103

Roger Casas
Estação do
Oriente, pp010-011
Padrão dos
Descobrimentos, p012
Igreja de Nossa Senhora do
Rosário de Fátima, p013
Museu Coleção
Berardo, p035
Restaurante Galeto, p044
Noobai Café, p050
Igreja de Nossa Senhora
Auxiliadora, p073
Fundação Calouste
Gulbenkian, pp074-075
Pavilhão de
Portugal, pp078-079
Luvaria Ulisses, p082
A Carioca, p086
Caza das Vellas
Loreto, p087
Hipódromo do Campo
Grande, pp090-091

Luís de Barros
Lisbon city view,
inside front cover

Nelson Garrido
Altis Belém Hotel &
Spa, p019, pp020-021
As Janelas Verdes,
p027, pp028-029
Padaria São Roque, p033
Orpheu Caffé, p047
Bistro 100 Maneiras, p055
Fábulas, pp056-057
Kais, p058
Zé dos Bois, pp060-061
Universidade Nova de
Lisboa, pp070-071
Véronique, pp084-085
Four Seasons Hotel
Ritz Spa, pp094-095
Casa Na Areia, p097

Fernando Guerra
L'And Vineyards, pp100-101

Daniel Malhão
Pedro e o Lobo,
pp048-049

João Morgado
Ponte 25 de
Abril, pp014-015
Fontecruz, p017
Four Seasons
Hotel Ritz, p026
Palácio Ramalhete,
pp030-031
A Vida Portuguesa, p034
Appleton Square,
pp036-037

Belcanto, p038, p039
SushiCafé Avenida, p041
Bica do Sapato, pp042-043
Tivoli Sky Bar, p045
Taberna da Rua das
Flores, p046
Cervejaria da
Esquina, p051
Lux Frágil, pp052-053
Casa Independente, p054
Largo, p059
Marco Balesteros, p063
Escola Superior de
Música, p065
Igreja do Sagrado Coração
de Jesus, pp066-067
Centro Ismaili, p068
Hotel Vitória, p069
Champalimaud Centre for
the Unknown, p072
Ler Devagar, p083
Longevity Wellness
Spa, p092, p093

Peartree Digital
Tricana tuna fillets, p081

António Sacchetti
Palácio Nacional da Pena,
pp098-099

LISBON
A COLOUR-CODED GUIDE TO THE HOT 'HOODS

PARTE ORIENTAL
Head north-east to Parque das Nações for a contemporary architecture showcase

GRAÇA/ALFAMA
These labyrinthine districts below the castle walls will transport you back in time

AMOREIRAS/CAMPO DE OURIQUE
The imposing Torres das Amoreiras stand out among commercial and residential blocks

RESTELO/ALCÂNTARA
An arty, leafy district on the riverbank with the Centro Cultural de Belém at its heart

LAPA/SANTOS
These upmarket areas combine ambassadors' palaces with some of Lisbon's finest shops

AVENIDAS NOVAS
Branching out from downtown, the 'new avenues' are lined with sought-after homes

BAIRRO ALTO/CHIADO
The city's party hub overlooks Chiado, a happy mix of old-school and cutting-edge retail

MONSANTO
A hilly Lisbon park that has the 19th-century Forte de Monsanto at its highest point

For a full description of each neighbourhood, see the Introduction.
Featured venues are colour-coded, according to the district in which they are located.